Cognitive Behavioral Therapy (CBT)

Quick Tips to Help Overcome Depression and Anxiety: Successful Stories That Give Hope to Regaining Control of Your Life

Introduction

Welcome to the book, *"Cognitive Behavioral Therapy (CBT): Quick Tips to Help Overcome Depression and Anxiety: Successful Stories That Give Hope to Regaining Control of Your Life"*.

This book contains proven steps and the best blueprint on how to overcome anxiety and depression using Cognitive Behavioral Therapy.

Do you have panic attacks and obsessive thoughts that make it difficult for you to live peacefully? Is your mind always occupied with unrelenting worries that cripple your ability to think clearly? Are there incapacitating phobias that rule your life and don't let you do things you want with ease? Do you feel withdrawn all the time and have lost all interest in life, especially the activities you once found meaningful and pleasurable?

If you answered yes to any of these questions, it is likely you are experiencing anxiety, depression, or maybe both. While you may feel as if you have been handed a death sentence, this isn't really the case. You really don't have to live a life characterized by anxiety and depression, and you can actually treat these conditions quite successfully provided you are committed to do so.

Each one of us is entitled to living a peaceful, meaningful and happy life. You too have that right and it is time you exercise it as well. Gear up for an insightful learning and find out how you can cure your anxiety and depression related issues for good with Cognitive Behavioral Therapy (CBT.)

Below are some examples that will help you figure out where your thought pattern stands before diving into the chapters:

Negative Thought Pattern

- Action: Michael walks through the cafeteria and stubs his toe on the table.

  Reaction: Lashes out and screams "Who the hell would put a table right here!"

  Emotional State: Becomes stressful and spirals downward to a phase of negative thoughts and victimhood.

- Action: Amy's car battery dies in the morning before heading to work.

  Reaction: "Of course this would happen to me on the day I have so much work to do at the office! Now my boss is going to think I am lying or overslept. I don't have the money to afford a new battery right now".

Emotional State: Highly overwhelmed/anxious due to lack of money and perceived negative confrontation with peers.

- Action: Kevin receives a car for a special milestone such as a birthday or anniversary.

Reaction: Temporary joy. Within a few hours or days, he will begin to think, "I did not want this car. I wanted the Mercedes". "Now I have to give a gift back because if I don't then I will look selfish". "Everyone is going to say I do not work hard for anything because I received this car as a gift. I do not want to deal with that pressure. I just want to give the car back. I will probably end up crashing it anyway knowing my bad luck."

Emotional State: Guilt/undue perceptions of what other will think causes social anxiety. Negative assumptions lead to negative results.

Positive Thought Pattern

- Action: Erica walks through the cafeteria and stubs her toe on the table.

Reaction: "Wow, I should really watch where I'm going". "How did I not see this table (laughing while in pain)".

Emotional State: Takes ownership of silly mistake. Does not take this mistake too serious which then makes it easy to move on and keep her emotional state at an even/heightened level.

- Action: Madison's car battery dies in the morning before heading to work.

  Reaction: "I have insurance or some other car service. I'll just call them and tell them I need some assistance." "I will call my boss and tell them I will be late. If they need proof of me buying a new battery, I will just show them the receipt". "Maybe my neighbors are home and can give me a quick jumpstart, so I can go get the battery replaced. I can be a few minutes late or stay late after work. Either way, at least I won't miss the whole day."

  Emotional State: Quick, spontaneous problem solving helps build confidence and stability. Emotional state rises once battery is replaced as he feels prepared to adjust to any situation thrown his way.

- Action: Tiffany receives a car for a special milestone such as a birthday or anniversary.

  Reaction: "I did want that Mercedes, but how can I complain? It's not everyday someone buys me a car". "I can't wait to drive this car". "I have the greatest friend/partner in the world. I can't wait to return the favor. They are going to love my gift as well".

Emotional State: Excited and gracious. Feels great about wanting to return the favor. More positive thinking breeds a healthy outlook on life.

If you have a negative thought pattern, you're in luck! With this book by your side and your efforts to follow the guidance in it consistently, you will soon get to a point where you live anxiety and depression-free and are happy with your life. If you have a positive thought pattern, you're also in luck. You will feel a sense of reassurance and learn a few extra tips to elevate your thoughts to the next level.

Respective authors own all copyrights not held by the publisher.

The information herein is offered for informational purposes solely, and is universal as so. The presentation of the information is without contract or any type of guarantee assurance.

The trademarks that are used are without any consent, and the publication of the trademark is without permission or backing by the trademark owner. All trademarks and brands within this book are for clarifying purposes only and are the owned by the owners themselves, not affiliated with this document.

Table of Contents

Chapter 1: Delving Into Anxiety And Depression

Your life is too precious and beautiful for you to let it slip from your hands just like that.

All of us become anxious and depressed occasionally, and some of us may even let that state linger on for quite some time. That said, eventually we do phase out of it, but there are some of us who no matter how hard they try or want cannot overcome that state at all.

If you are currently going through that phase where your depressing fears, inexorable concerns, compulsive thoughts and debilitating fears are getting the better of you, you know how hard it is to battle those feelings.

Having said that, the good news is you have a cure to your problems waiting for you to tap into it. CBT is indeed an effective procedure to cure anxiety and depression to reclaim your life once again.

However, before moving on to discussing how that can be done, let us quickly have an overview of what anxiety and depression are and the differences between the two followed by an understanding of CBT in the next chapter.

Anxiety and Depression- How Similar are they?

Often, anxiety and depression are used interchangeably. If you ask someone the difference between the two, it is likely he/ she won't know it unless he/ she is well aware of the conditions and has studied psychology.

While some people aren't fully aware of the conditions at all, this misconception that anxiety and depression are the same also stems from the fact that around 50% people diagnosed with depression also suffer from anxiety, and vice versa.

That said; if you want to properly and effectively treat your condition, it is crucial to understand exactly what you are going through so you reach a proper diagnosis and can then opt for the right techniques to cure your problem. For that, it is only right to have a clear understanding of anxiety and depression, and how the two are similar and different.

Understanding Anxiety and Depression

Anxiety refers to the feeling of overwhelm, nervousness, uneasiness or worry you experience before something important, dominating, threatening or upsetting. It is your body's very natural and normal response to anything it finds stressful. The feeling you get on the first day of your job or before taking an examination or before addressing a huge crowd is what anxiety, feels like.

Whenever you encounter or are about to encounter any situation that feels stressful to you, your brain activates the stress response in your body. Aka the 'fight, flight or freeze' response, this response produces certain physiological changes in your body including the release of hormones such as cortisol that increase your stress and make you cope with the pressure by fighting it, fleeing it or in extreme situations, freezing in it.

This is the response that helps you escape a fight or run hard when you see a snake approaching you or instantly apply brakes of your car when an old lady suddenly appears on the road. This response is what makes you feel anxious before or during nerve wrecking situations and handle them effectively.

While it is normal and in fact essential to experience this response in times of need, if your anxiety lasts for a long time, does not dissipate even after a couple of months and starts to interfere with your routine life, you are likely to suffer from one or the other form of anxiety disorder.

As opposed to this, depression is feeling withdrawn, dejected, lonely and upset for over 2 weeks. While anxiety manifests itself as a type of worry mostly pertinent to the future, depression encompasses feeling lonely and disappointed mostly about something that happened in the past.

Also, depressed people mostly feel that only bad things will happen to them no matter what. While in anxiety, it is an uncertainty that upsets you, if you are depressed, you are sure that you are doomed for good. Depression doesn't make you worry, but comes with the sense of confirmation that only bad things will happen to you.

Apart from this, the physical manifestations of both anxiety and depression are different as well. Depression usually brings with it changes in appetite and weight, sleep issues including both insomnia and sleeping too much, pains including headaches, shoulder aches and backaches and digestion problems.

On the other hand, anxiety carries with it problems like increased heart rate, hyperventilation, profuse sweating and bowel issues. Some of the physical manifestations of anxiety are similar to those of a heart attack, which is why often people confuse panic attacks with heart attacks.

Apart from the differences, the two share, both conditions are quite closely linked too. When you worry relentlessly, you are likely to seclude yourself from everyone else, which can make you feel lonely and dejected and can lead to depression. Similarly, if depressed, you can start to worry a lot about what may happen to you if you stay engulfed in depression for long. This can then switch on your anxious mode. There are two very important things I want you to remember as we move forward. One, you are NOT alone in this struggle. Two, because you are not alone, and many others experience similar battles, that means there are also plenty of avenues to seek treatment. So travel down this road with me as we discuss one of the most prominent forms of treatment, next.

Chapter 2: How CBT Cures Anxiety And Depression

The extensive field of psychology has experienced a great deal of improvement and advancement over the past few decades and has shifted towards the use of more evidence-based practices including the use of CBT to treat a number of emotional and psychological issues. Study after study proves that CBT is indeed a brilliant way to treat health issues including anxiety and depression. Let us learn a little bit more about cognitive behavioral therapy (CBT) to know what makes it effective in treating various health conditions including anxiety and depression.

What is CBT

As quite evident from its name, Cognitive Behavioral Therapy aka CBT revolves around your cognition and behavior. Focusing on how you think and act, CBT is rooted in the notion that your thoughts pertinent to a certain situation greatly and directly affect how you feel, both physically and emotionally which then influences and shapes the way you behave in that very situation and even afterwards.

It is one of our innate needs and tendencies to associate meaning(s) to everything that happens around us. Therefore, if someone lost something or if you saw a fight on the road, you are likely to think something about that incident and associate some sort of meaning to it. While you do that, there are others interpreting those events as well; and since everyone is different, it is quite likely that two people interpret the same event differently.

For instance, if two friends go to a party, one may find it boring while it is possible the other finds it engaging and interesting. The same activities going on in the party can easily be perceived as different by two or more people attending it. The same happens to you when you are engulfed with anxiety or depression, or even both. The situation that has affected you or triggered your condition may not be as sabotaging to others as it is to you, but since you have been greatly influenced by it, it is important to analyze your behavior and cognition to reach a better understanding of the problem. In addition, never compare your emotional reactions to someone else's. Focus on how you feel and do not feel ashamed. We all have different strengths and weaknesses. The stories used above are just here to serve as examples.

Now let us dig deeper into how CBT can help with curing anxiety and depression.

CBT to the Rescue

CBT is by far the most commonly used therapy procedure to treat anxiety and depression related disorders and research has proven it quite effectual in treating phobias, panic attacks and clinical depression. Here is how it does the trick.

- Helps Examine Your Thought Process: CBT is divided into two main parts: cognitive and behavioral therapy. As mostly, anxiety and depression disorders are rooted in your negative thoughts and how you emotionally react to different situations, it is important to examine your thought process to better understand how they contributed to your condition. The cognitive therapy helps you do just that by exploring and digging deeper into your thought process primarily the negative thoughts to comprehend their effect on your behavior, emotions and life. This helps identify the glitches in your mind that keep triggering your problem and never let you sit peacefully. When the glitches are fixed properly, the negative thoughts, fears and concerns are replaced by positive thoughts, assurances and beliefs that influence your life positively and help you gain stability. Then, instead of using your precious, emotional capital on trying to solve the way you feel, you may rather properly address and solve the *problem*.

- Assists in Understanding Your Behavior Better: The behavioral therapy helps you examine your behavior and how you react or respond to different changes, situations and experiences. This knowledge gives insight into your triggers so you learn to manage them better. For instance, if meeting a friend who keeps telling you how successful you were a few years back and how you have lost that touch now triggers your anxiety and makes you lock yourself in the room for hours, it clearly shows that the friend triggers your anxiety. When you get insight into your behavior, you know what affects you a certain way and you can then bring appropriate changes to your environment.

- Enables You to Improve Your Perception of Things: In reality, it is not situations or people who trigger your depression or anxiety, but your perception of different elements and experiences that sets the conditions off. If you perceive a financial setback as a death sentence, it is likely to make you feel depressed. However, if you perceive it as an unfortunate experience whose effect will eventually fade away, faster if you work harder, you won't let it influence you much. CBT provides you with detailed understanding of how your reactions and responses elicit different results and how you need to improve your perception of things to live better. This understanding helps you live in the moment and not make a mountain out of a molehill because that will only affect your mind negatively.

When you learn to think positively, perceive things neutrally and positively and respond to them calmly, you are able to slowly assuage and then overcome your anxiety and depression and move on to live a happy, peaceful life. Let us go through the different techniques you can work on to achieve that in the chapters to follow.

Chapter 3: Challenge Your Thoughts

If you dig deeper into both, anxiety and depression, you will realize that both the disorders mostly stem from negative thoughts that were given far too much importance. If you keep thinking on how something silly you said made you look like a fool in front of your friends, you are likely to trigger your anxiety, which may then lead to depression. Similarly, if you keep reminiscing all the times your partner said hurtful things to you and how he called you 'mental', you would soon feel sure that you are crazy and do not deserve love which would then make you fall into the excruciating pit of depression.

One way or the other, it is your negative thoughts and your constant rumination of them that sets off your disorders. How you react to different situations, perceive them and let your thoughts run wild in all sorts of unhealthy directions is what corrupts your mind.

To get better control of yourself and condition, this behavior needs to be corrected. For that, you need to learn the art of being aware of and then challenge your unhealthy thoughts. Here is how you can do that:

Be Aware of Your Thoughts

For you to learn to challenge a thought, you first need to identify it. Oftentimes, we aren't even fully aware of what we are thinking primarily because we are so accustomed to think of a gazillion things at the same time. So while you are typing on your laptop, you may also be thinking of the electricity bill you have to pay and the coat you have to collect from the drycleaners and the 4pm seminar you have to attend today.

Amidst all of that, there are countless emotions deep seated in your mind that are manipulating all your thoughts, emotions and feelings. If you aren't aware of them, chances are you allow an unhealthy emotion to sit in your mind for far too long only to influence your thoughts negatively. You may not even realize how you have been thinking on how a colleague made fun of your shoes and how that thought is slowly eating away on your confidence crippling it to the extent that it triggers your anxiety.

To keep negative thoughts from blowing out of proportion and affecting your sanity, start being more aware of how you think, feel and react to things. Remember, you are not meant to hold on to each thought you experience especially the unhealthy ones and if you start grabbing onto them firmly, they will only cripple you emotionally, psychologically and soon physically. Here is how you can keep that from happening:

- When working or doing anything else even if it is just lying on the bed, focus only on the one thought that you are thinking. If you are thinking about how your body feels on the bed or planning what you will speak about in your presentation, think about that only. If any other thought, pops up, remind yourself of what you were thinking earlier and get back to that thought. Even if a thought is only 3 seconds long, devote those 3 seconds to it alone and move to another thought once the previous one has been completed. It is going to take you quite some time to train yourself to focus only on one thought at a time, but if you stay consistent with the practice, you will get there.

- As you start becoming more aware of your thoughts, you will be able to spot the negative ones faster too. Focus on the emotions associated with every thought and the emotions it stirs up inside you when you think of it. So if you think about how you may fail in an examination, concentrate on the emotions it elicits inside you. If the emotions bring about negativity, anger, frustration or any other emotion that upsets you, the thought is likely to be a negative one and you need to take care of it immediately.

- You need to analyze the importance of the thought and then challenge it accordingly. For instance, if you are thinking about how you can never live happily because you have no loved one, are jobless and sinking in debts, and this thought is constantly lowering your happiness, confidence and sanity, you need to challenge it and replace it with something more realistic and positive.

- To challenge it, question its authenticity by finding any evidence that supports it and then test out its reality. If you think you are doomed for life and will forever be miserable, think about any time in your life when you were truly happy. If you can find out even one such incident, it shows you are capable of being happy and it is the recent events that have affected you negatively. Similarly, if you are thinking of a future concern that is sabotaging your wellbeing, question the possibility of it actually happening. If you think you will never find a good life partner, ask yourself the odds of that happening. Keep asking yourself questions shaped positively so your mind comes up with positive answers to that. Instead of asking, 'Will I never find true love?' ask yourself 'Do I have a chance of finding love because I did fall in love once before?' Your mind is designed to answer questions exactly in the manner you propose them so if you ask positively constructed questions, you will get positive answers in exchange.

- Next, replace that negative thought with something structured in a more realistic and positive manner. So if you thought 'I am going to fail the next job interview too', change it to something like 'I can do well in the job interview if I brush up on my confidence and knowledge of the job.' If you think about how your life is a death sentence, tell yourself that 'Life is a series of ups and downs, and if today is a bad day, it won't remain that way for good especially if I stop holding onto it.' If you start doing that consistently and keep speaking positively to yourself, you will start to get out of the depressive, anxious phase. Your thoughts shape your beliefs and mindset, and if you think about something for far too long, it leaves an influence on your mind and a taste in your mouth. Naturally, if you were to tell yourself how pathetic you are or how unfair life is to you, you will feel and experience that. If you change that to how things can be better if I think positively and hold onto that thought, things will certainly improve.

Remember that working on these guidelines once isn't enough. Any practice influences you and your life if you nurture a habit of it. Hence, you just don't have to challenge a negative thought once and replace it with a positive thought occasionally, but you need to build habits of these practices. Work on these practices consistently so you train yourself to always behave realistically and positively so a negative thought doesn't gain ground in your mind.

Also, you need to understand that everything is meant to pass on in this life. Even human beings are meant to be born, live and then die. Nothing is immortal and that is the reality of life. Why is it then you let a negative thought to stay forever in your mind, at least for the time you are alive? Why do you allow it to become immortal when it is supposed to live for a few seconds only?

When a negative thought keeps popping up in your head time again and starts to rattle your mind, remind yourself of the fact that nothing lasts for good and you must not hold onto that thought if you want it to pass away.

To stop holding onto an unwanted thought, distract yourself with other activities when it persists even after you have replaced it with something positive. Sometimes, leaving the room, you are in and doing something else does the trick so try these approaches.

You now need to consistently and religiously work on these strategies for them to yield positive results. In addition, you need to learn to calm yourself the minute something unfortunate, unexpected or upsetting happens. If you are going to have a panic attack every time a negative thought strikes you, you are quite likely to exacerbate your condition instead of assuaging it.

Jake, 38 is a HR manager who is now living a well-balanced life, but things were different for him about 4 years back. He suffered a major episode of depression when he lost his job, went under massive debt and went through an ugly divorce. He used to stay in his room all day long and stopped meeting his friends too. Luckily, he was saved by a friend who encouraged him to use CBT.

CBT helped him realize that negative thoughts and holding negative perceptions of every day and even big experiences leads to depression. He did go through some bad episodes in life and instead of learning from them, and getting back up after some time, he accepted them as declarations of his failure and stopped even trying to improve things. He became so engulfed in negative thoughts that he found it nearly impossible to step out of that whirlpool. With the help of the technique discussed above, he learnt how to recognize and challenge negative thoughts to curb his depression and slowly overcome it.

It took him about 6 months to end the vicious cycle of negative thoughts that kept pulling him towards depression, but eventually he was able to accomplish that goal. He has now quite a good control of his thoughts and stays aware of them to keep a check on his changing mood and onset of depression.

To be able to calmly respond to things and be able to consciously analyze your thoughts, you need to learn to calm yourself down. The next chapter shares with you some tricks to do just that.

If you are enjoying this book, would you be kind enough to leave a review on Amazon because I would like to hear how the book has improved your life. If you make it to the last page of this book and did not enjoy its value, publisher details will be given to inform what could have been done to better serve your expectations.

Chapter 4: Keeping Your Anxiety Attacks And Depression In Control

The minute your brain receives a signal that something traumatizing or upsetting is going to happen, it sets off your stress response and your anxiety is quite likely to go berserk then. You need to be able to calm yourself down when something upsetting strikes you so you can mitigate your anxiousness and depression appropriately instead of allowing it to get the better of you. This is how you learn to keep your negative thoughts from wreaking havoc in your mind. Here is what you need to do for that to happen.

Take Deep Breaths

Studies prove that one of the biggest triggers of panic attacks is rapid, shallow breath. It is perceived as a sign of threat and when your brain registers that, it sets off your fight, flight or freeze response only to aggravate your anxiousness. When this happens, your mind is likely to go berserk too and your ability to stay in control of your thoughts is likely to weaken.

A good way to keep the problem from exacerbating is to quickly calm down your anxious mind the minute you register that. If you have been working on staying aware of yourself and your thoughts, you would now be able to identify when a certain thought or experience makes you feel depressed or anxious. The moment you acknowledge that, start taking deep, calming breaths to release your in-built anxiety.

- Make a conscious effort to inhale through your nose to a count of 4, 5 or 6.

- It will be difficult for you, but encourage yourself to focus only on how the air enters through your nose and the way the breath feels inside you. Pay attention to how your belly extends when you inhale and any other movement that you can sense in your body.

- Hold that breath to another count of 4, 5 or 6 and focus on the feeling you experience then.

- Gently, release the breath through your mouth to a final count of 4, 5 or 6. Push it out of your body and pay attention to the movements produced in your body as a result.

- Practice this for 5 to 10 breaths and throughout that time, gently encourage yourself to focus on the breath alone and nothing else. This too, is going to be a tough job for now since focusing on one thing at a time does not come easy to many of us, but keep trying.

Work on this strategy consistently and try to practice breathing using this technique throughout the day. This way you will slowly train yourself to take conscious, slow and deep breaths and keep random anxiety at bay. Also, you will gain better control of your racing mind, which is often the reason why you overthink things and trigger anxiety or depression. Another thing you need to understand is that taking conscious, deep breaths is a behavior as well, one that you work on every day to change the way you perceive things.

Emily, 25 is a techie and a blogger who suffered from chronic anxiety a year ago. She realized that she didn't have a strong control on her racing thoughts which made her think and assume the negative case scenario of everything.

After taking CBT treatment for her problem, she learned the art of taking deep breaths and being aware of her thoughts and that has helped her get back in the driver's seat of her life. She has now better control of her anxiety as she resorts to deep breathing every time she feels her breath becoming rapid. This calms her down making her focus better on her thoughts.

Stay Put

Remember to stay very strong when a panic attack or bout of depression hits you hard. The moment you observe yourself becoming too low, stressed, nervous or frustrated, remind yourself that this is just a phase and will pass away. Overthinking the situation and telling yourself repeatedly of how you are anxious or depressed is often the practice that worsens the condition.

Stay put during that phase and tell yourself of how everything is going to be perfectly fine. Keep saying 'I am okay and have things under control' repeatedly to yourself loudly and slowly. This practice is also known as 'chanting positive affirmations' and is a good way to rewire your brain to think positively and focus on positive things instead of negative ones. Try this a few times and you will soon learn how to keep your negativity in check through the power of words.

Observe Your Triggers

As you start to become calmer and more self-aware with time, take this awareness up a notch and use it to understand your triggers better. You need to know exactly what sets off your depression or anxiety so you can better manage those triggers.

Be conscious of yourself throughout the day and look for any change in your emotions, thoughts and feelings as you engage in one activity after another. The moment you feel a certain activity, experience, object or person makes you feel differently, take note of that. You then need to observe it closely and as nonjudgmentally as possible. This means that you need to try not to attach any sort of ill feelings or negative labels to the trigger and perceive it as just an experience that makes you feel in an undesirable manner.

Once you become better aware of your triggers, you need to manage them appropriately so they don't intensify your condition. For instance, if being late to work infuriates your boss who then shouts at you which leads to an episode of depression, try to reach work on time. Similarly, if you know, being around certain people can upset you; distance yourself from them for some time until you get better control of your condition.

Nathan 29 is a pharmacist who suffered from generalized anxiety disorder about 2 years ago. He used to worry incessantly about things that weren't even going to happen and kept thinking about how things will never work in his favor all the time. With the help of CBT, he learnt to observe his triggers and realized that often it was being around a negative influence and seeing others experience setbacks in life that triggered his negative thoughts and led to anxiety. He is now quite stable emotionally and has learnt to keep his anxiety under check.

Record Your Behaviors

Next, you need to start keeping track of your behaviors especially in response to your anxiety/ depression triggers so you know how you take on those triggers. What is it that a certain trigger makes you do? Does it make you go under the covers and stay there for the entire day or do you keep thinking excessively for hours or do you stop taking calls and messages to disconnect yourself from the outside world?

Being aware of your behaviors is important so you can identify meaningful activities that you can engage in during that time to manage your anxiety and depression. Also, your behaviors help you understand the extent to which your condition affects you. As you become better aware of that, you realize how anxiety and depression influences and sabotages your life and why you must battle it.

Upon working on these strategies for some time, you will start experiencing a reduction in your heightened anxiety and depression. You now need to work on meaningful activities to quickly curb your anxiety and depression for good.

Chapter 5: Curbing Anxiety And Depression Through Positive Behaviors

Often, anxiety and depression stem from not feeling good and confident about yourself. When you lack the courage to meet people and interact with them, your social anxiety is likely to intensify. Similarly, if you keep failing one job interview after another, your depression could prolong for a long time.

At this point, you need to work on different activities in a manner that you face your fears and prove your anxiety and depression wrong every time.

Practice Systematic Desensitization

Systematic desensitization involves slowly facing your fears and exposing yourself to things that trigger your anxiety and depression. You need to do that gradually so you don't overwhelm yourself and flip off your anxiety/ depression switch.

Make a note of all the things that you are afraid of or those that make you feel unhappy and then devise a detailed plan on how to slowly take on those challenges. If you have a cleaning OCD (obsessive-compulsive disorder), don't just stop washing your hands instantly. Instead, slowly cut back on your time spent in the bathroom wiping off invisible dirt off your body. If you do it for 2 hours every time you enter the bathroom, cut back on it with 10 minutes every day. Similarly, if you are depressed because your business is failing, identify its weak areas and slowly start working on them.

Before you put this information to use and leave a review for this book on Amazon, let me give you one last bonus piece of information that I personally use when I feel overwhelmed with negative emotion. I call it the "separation method". Let's say, I graduated from college and I was awarded grant money during my education. A few months after, I get a letter in the mail from the government claiming that I must refund thousands of dollars because I made a mistake and put the wrong number of siblings that lived in my household which is one of reasons I was awarded the grant. Here are my thoughts. "They're lying!". "Did I really make that stupid mistake?". "I have to pay this money on top of student loans!" These are my emotions: worried, stressed, angry, regretful, and whatever emotion fits best for "the world is against me". Here are the possible solutions: pay the money, argue with the government employees all day (which really only intensifies stress and I eventually pay the money after requesting to see the documents), do not pay the money and eventually be sued. This is all a true story by the way, but the next part is what you will take with you and apply it to whatever problems you have. Take notes.

My thoughts, emotions, and possible outcomes are now separated. Next, it is up to me to make a decision. Will I allow myself to healthily, whole-heartedly, and deeply feel whatever emotions have arisen for fifteen minutes only and then to let it pass instead of fighting it? Do I just say, "eh fuck it, what happened is not in my control, but what happens next *is* in my control so let's go solve this problem and move on"? Or, do I just totally switch up my perspective and begin to laugh out loud at how small this problem is knowing that it will not be of any importance whatsoever in a day, week, month, or year? I will let you choose.

Conclusion

I hope this book provided you with the value you were looking for and serves as your guide that takes you towards recovery and improvement just like CBT did for many others like you. It takes time, patience and consistency to yield positive results and you need to stay strong throughout that time. If you keep working on your goal consistently, soon enough you will surely overcome anxiety and depression.

Please remember to leave your review on Amazon if you enjoyed this book. Thank you and always strive to continue growing!

www.ingramcontent.com/pod-product-compliance
Lightning Source LLC
Chambersburg PA
CBHW061546250726
48657CB00006B/2319